"I resolved many years ago that it was my obligation to break the cycle—that if I could be anything in life, I would be a good father to my girls; that if I could give them anything, I would give them that rock—that foundation—on which to build their lives. And that would be the greatest gift I could offer."

THE GREATEST GIFT
I COULD OFFER

QUOTATIONS FROM
BARACK OBAMA
ON
PARENTING
AND FAMILY

, OLIVIA M. CLOUD ,

BERKLEY BOOKS, NEW YORK

THE BERKLEY PUBLISHING GROUP
Published by the Penguin Group
Penguin Group (USA) Inc.
375 Hudson Street, New York, New York 10014, USA
Penguin Group (Canada), 90 Eglinton Avenue East, Suite 700, Toronto, Ontario M4P 2Y3, Canada
(a division of Pearson Penguin Canada Inc.)
Penguin Books Ltd., 80 Strand, London WC2R 0RL, England
Penguin Group Ireland, 25 St. Stephen's Green, Dublin 2, Ireland (a division of Penguin Books Ltd.)
Penguin Group (Australia), 250 Camberwell Road, Camberwell, Victoria 3124, Australia
(a division of Pearson Australia Group Pty. Ltd.)
Penguin Books India Pvt. Ltd., 11 Community Centre, Panchsheel Park, New Delhi—110 017, India
Penguin Group (NZ), 67 Apollo Drive, Rosedale, North Shore 0632, New Zealand
(a division of Pearson New Zealand Ltd.)
Penguin Books (South Africa) (Pty.) Ltd., 24 Sturdee Avenue, Rosebank, Johannesburg 2196,
South Africa

Penguin Books Ltd., Registered Offices: 80 Strand, London WC2R 0RL, England

This book is an original publication of The Berkley Publishing Group.

First edition: April 2009

Berkley trade paperback ISBN: 978-0-425-23140-1

PRINTED IN THE UNITED STATES OF AMERICA

10 9 8 7 6 5 4 3 2 1

Most Berkley books are available at special quantity discounts for bulk purchases for sales promotions,
premiums, fund-raising, or educational use. Special books, or book excerpts, can also be created to fit
specific needs. For details, write: Special Markets, Penguin Group (USA) Inc., 375 Hudson Street,
New York, New York 10014.

CONTENTS

INTRODUCTION

I N LESS THAN two years, Barack Obama has become a national symbol of hope. His historic victory on November 4, 2008, is for many the fulfillment of a dream long held. An emerging icon of change, President Obama is the embodiment of the American Dream. Repeatedly, he has said of himself, "In no other country on earth is my story even possible." It is precisely because Obama's life story is such an unlikely one that he has emerged as a transformative figure.

Without a doubt, Obama is a phenomenal man who represents a changing landscape in America. However, to most of us, he is also a regular guy. Raised primarily by a single mother and her parents, our 44th president is a man of simple mid-America roots. He is the son who grew up without a father, but who made his mother proud. He is the husband who forgets to pick up his socks off the bedroom floor, but is madly in love with his wife. He is the father who attends parent-teacher conferences and still finds time to read *Harry Potter* to his daughters.

People love Barack Obama because he has the vision and humility to be a leader of the free world. He also demonstrates empathy for those he has been elected to serve. He knows what it means to repay student loans. He understands the struggles of living within a household budget. He even knows what it feels like to have his credit card declined. His experiences, about which he has been forthright, are those with which the majority of Americans can relate.

Barack Obama demonstrates a commitment to family that is not promoted to impress a voting public; but rather, his commitment is that of a true family man. When he left the campaign trail to visit his grandmother just weeks before the election, many pundits questioned whether his absence would hurt the campaign. Yet, he chose a few final moments with his dying grandmother over the possibility of a few lost votes.

There are other reminders of his devotion to family: the touching picture of his mother-in-law, Marian Robinson, holding his hand as they watched the election returns; the announcement that she would be coming to live with them in the White House to help Michelle look after the girls; and the biggest news of all—Malia and Sasha's new puppy!

In October 2008, I had an opportunity to briefly meet the Obamas after the second presidential debate hosted by Nashville's Belmont University. As the one of a chosen few "town hall" debate delegates, I had an opportunity to see beyond the television camera's eye. As the debate ensued, I took a moment to pan our surroundings. I looked beyond one section of delegates and suppressed the urge to gasp when I saw Michelle Obama. I don't know why I was surprised to see her. I suppose it was because no one told us she would be there.

Then, only for a second, I caught a glimpse of her mouthing a quick message to her husband. I couldn't make out the words, but her lip movements and eye contact were quite deliberate and focused toward him. Her actions were quick and discreet. The brief incident was fascinating primarily because Michelle's actions were typical of what any supportive spouse would do for a partner about to venture onto the stage.

At that moment, it occurred to me that there were eighty delegates and about 1,000 spectators watching the debate in that room, plus an estimated sixty-three million more nationwide. But with all those people watching, including senators, representatives, celebrities, and a former vice president, Barack Obama's eyes locked in to one person at that critical moment—his wife.

I'll never know the content of that quickly mouthed message, but here's something I did come to understand during my debate experience: the Obamas are a real family; they're a real married couple. She wants to help him do his best and, in turn, her opinion matters to him.

Following the debate, we were allowed to take pictures. After having successfully maneuvered pictures with the Obamas separately, I wanted more—a shot with the two of them. I asked

Michelle if she thought she could use her wifely influence to get him to stop for a pose. She surveyed the crowd, found her husband across the room, and immediately but graciously assessed that she could not accommodate my request. I was disappointed, but her response reflected a wife who knows her husband. She knew he was in his zone, talking with voters about their concerns, answering questions, and giving photo ops.

My brief encounter with the Obamas led me on the journey of this book. During the debate, I was intrigued by his response to what Tom Brokaw called a "Zen-like" question: "What don't you know and how will you learn it?" Barack quickly pointed to Michelle as the person who could probably best tell what he did not know.

Many times, I've reflected on that encounter, as well as Obama's numerous comments regarding families—from expressing his concern over the spiraling economy's impact on the family to his frustration over watching his mother battle with the insurance company regarding her illness—and I am encouraged. I know beyond a shadow of a doubt that the American family has a true ally in the White House.

What is inspiring about President Obama is that he has always made it a priority to publicly voice his commitment to his wife and daughters, to connect his own family experiences to America's families, and to share his philosophies about what family truly means. This commitment to family is poignantly reflected in his profound speeches, in his media interviews, and in his books, *Dreams from My Father* and *The Audacity of Hope*. In sharing his words, I hope they will be as enriching and insightful to you as they are to me.

Olivia M. Cloud

"Of all the rocks upon which we build our lives, we are reminded today that family is the most important."

TO HOLD THINGS TOGETHER

MICHELLE GREW UP with a dad who was an exemplary model of devotion and responsibility, while most of what Barack knows of his father was gleaned from letters and stories from his mother and grandparents.

Despite their diverse upbringings, the first couple formed a loving bond based on a mutual desire to build a strong family. Michelle wants a good husband and father in her own family because she knows what that feels like and how important it is. Barack wants the same, precisely because he *didn't* have his father in his life and deeply desires to give to his daughters what he missed.

It's apparent that Michelle and Barack are a team, even if at times the partnership seems a little more one-sided. But most marriages are like that. Even partners in the best, most solid unions at some point have to do the hard work of finding balance and rhythm in their relationship for the sake of the entire family.

"I know what it means when you don't have a strong male figure in the house, which is why the hardest thing about me being in politics sometimes is not being home as much as I'd like, and I'm just blessed that I've got such a wonderful wife at home to hold things together."

21ST-CENTURY STANDARDS

PARENTS HAVE ASPIRATIONS and high hopes for their children, like a college degree and a career that will securely provide for their own family some day. Preparation for that success means taking full advantage of all that is offered in school as well as the knowledge beyond classroom walls.

Few children will have the same opportunities for world exposure as Malia and Sasha, but parents can expand their own children's opportunities by exposing the entire family to diverse cultures in their own community.

Mothers and fathers can encourage their children's interest in different countries and languages to prepare them to deal with people who are different from themselves, much in the same way that Barack's diverse upbringing has equipped him to deal with a broad cross section of people.

Every parent is not well versed in technology, but every parent can inspire their children's ambitions by insuring they are gaining a workable knowledge of the kinds of competencies that will guide them to future success.

"We're living in a 21st-century knowledge economy, but our schools, our homes, and our culture are still based around 20th-century expectations . . . we need to start setting high standards and inspirational examples for our children to follow."

ROCK OF THE OBAMA FAMILY

B ARACK OBAMA MAY be the most powerful man in the world right now, but there's one person who has more power than him—Michelle Obama. It was she alone who held what she termed *veto power* regarding his decision to run for president.

The Obamas attribute the success of their marriage, in part, to Barack's sensitivity to the sacrifices Michelle makes in order to make his political career possible. He appreciates all the things she does in his absence, aware that her job is often challenging.

Michelle Obama's openness about her challenges serves as an inspiration to many women who juggle work and family while maintaining a healthy marriage. While she quickly debunks the supermom myth, our First Lady adeptly manages it in a way that earns her the respect of the nation and the world.

Mothers are powerful.

❝ *I've seen my wife, Michelle, the rock of the Obama family, juggling work and parenting with more skill and grace than anyone I know.* **❞**

INSPIRING OUR CHILDREN

MICHELLE RECALLED PEOPLE cheering as she walked the girls to class on the day after the election. Meanwhile, Malia's response to all the fanfare was, "*That's* embarrassing." She told her dad she didn't care about being really, really rich. What was more important to her was having a simple life. But the children of the first African American president will have lives that are anything but simple.

At some point, the girls will have settled into a measure of routine—meeting new friends, adjusting to a new school, and doing homework. In that regard, their lives are no different from other children whose parent got a new job requiring relocation.

While the magnitude of being members of the first family may now elude young Malia and Sasha, their parents are rearing them to recognize their own sense of purpose. They will certainly be raised with a sense of the responsibility that a life of privilege commands.

"To do this, we must start by inspiring our children with a sense of purpose . . . by nurturing their imagination so that they may dream big and then work hard to reach those dreams.**"**

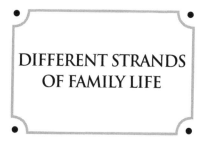

DIFFERENT STRANDS
OF FAMILY LIFE

bamalot IS A term some are using to describe the charm and grace of America's first couple. Their relationship is a throwback to the nation's first couple in the year that Barack was born. John and Jacqueline Kennedy's relationship had a charismatic quality, much like the relationship between President Obama and his First Lady.

But the magical relationship that America sees is the product of commitment, determination, compromise, and of course, love.

In the early years of the Obamas' marriage, they worked through the struggles and strains that have caused lesser couples to break. From all accounts, their conflicts were no different than those most couples face. When two people marry, they have to learn to live together, accept each other's quirks and idiosyncrasies, and respect each other's space.

The Obama marriage is strong because the ties that bind them are strong—love, family, and hope for the future.

"We represent two strands of family life in this country—the strand that is very stable and solid, and then the strand that is breaking out of the constraints of traditional families, traveling, separated, mobile. I think there was that strand in me of imagining what it would be like to have a stable, solid, secure family life."

THE SAME OPPORTUNITIES

FROM THE START, Barack was attracted to Michelle for many reasons—her beauty, her resourcefulness, her humor, and her intelligence.

She was strictly a career-minded lady when they met, but by his own admission, he wore her down until she agreed to go on a date with him. Without question, she is grooming her daughters to be equally smart, successful women in their own right.

During their time in the White House, Malia and Sasha will be exposed to the best education, both within and outside the classroom. World leaders will be entertained in their home and they will commune with nature on the secluded grounds of Camp David.

With all that their upbringing will prepare them to do, and the advances their father's presidency could make for women, those beautiful little girls will, we hope, grow up in a world where gender bias is viewed as obsolete as the idea that there could never be a black president.

*" I want my daughters to have a choice as to what's best
for them and their families. Whether they will have such
choices will depend not just on their own efforts and at-
titudes. As Michelle has taught me, it will also depend
on men—and American society—respecting and
accommodating the choices they make. "*

IF KIDS KNOW
THEY'RE LOVED

THE ANNOUNCEMENT THAT the girls would be getting a dog was one of their father's most important and touching points during his historic election night speech in Chicago's Grant Park.

When the announcement was made that the girls had earned their new puppy, people were *almost* as excited for the girls as they were for Obama's victory. It wasn't just his victory; it was the girls' victory, too. They were at the center of things!

Michelle and Barack work hard to give their children a life of normalcy—genuine family times, real friendships with schoolmates, attending church, and involvement in the community. Stability is important to the Obamas—Michelle always had a stable family life and knows how important it is, while the president did *not* have much stability growing up and yearned for it. Yet, the essential ingredient each of them had, in very different kinds of families, was love.

> "I've always believed that if kids know they're loved, if they know that in their parents' eyes they are special, that can make up for a lot of instability and a lot of . . . change."

AN IDEAL HUSBAND
AND FATHER

I n *The Audacity of Hope*, Barack tells of a phone call he made to Michelle in Chicago from his Washington, DC, office. He was particularly excited about a piece of legislation he co-sponsored that had a very good chance of passing.

She cut him off with the news that their kitchen and bathroom had been invaded by ants. He was to pick up ant traps on the way home. In her own amusing way, Michelle reminded Barack that despite his many successes, the family's well-being is the number one priority.

A real home life doesn't have superstars. The work of being a family goes on and on. No matter how busy or important one parent's job may be, a marriage has to be a partnership—for the sake of the relationship and for the sake of the children.

"My wife has been my closest friend, my closest advisor. . . . She's not somebody who looks to the limelight, or even is wild about me being in politics. And that's a good reality check on me. When I go home, she wants me to be a good father and a good husband. And everything else is secondary to that."

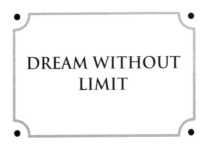

DREAM WITHOUT LIMIT

AMERICA SMILED AS Malia and Sasha greeted their father via telecast after Michelle's speech at the 2008 Democratic National Convention. To the world, the man on the JumboTron was the Democratic nominee for president, but to the Obama girls, he was just "daddy."

As Michelle and the girls exited the stage, a band played to the tune of "Mighty Love," an old-school song by The Spinners. Anyone who witnessed the exchange understood that theirs was indeed a mighty love—between Barack and Michelle and between an ambitious father and his adoring daughters.

Obama is aware that his time with his family is far too short and precious. If he completes a second term, Malia will be ready for college and Sasha will soon be going on her first date.

His love for his daughters makes him all the more sensitive to the goals he and Michelle have for them—the goals that all parents have for their children.

"I thought about the world that Sasha and Malia will grow up in, about the chances they'll have and the challenges they'll face. And I thought about my hopes for them—that they'll be able to dream without limit, achieve without constraint, and be free to seek their own happiness.**"**

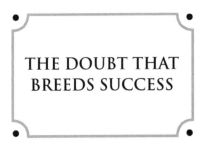

THE DOUBT THAT
BREEDS SUCCESS

I T'S NORMAL FOR even the best of parents to question or second-guess themselves. When gauging our own competence, whether as a parent, or spouse, or other roles in life, it's usually easier to determine our successes in retrospect. When we're in the process, the task just seems hard and it causes us to question our capabilities.

The responsibilities of marriage, parenting, and being an involved family member are very important. We don't have long, in the scheme of things, to do it; yet, our impact can be felt for generations to come.

It's interesting that, of all Obama's accomplishments, the responsibilities that cause him to doubt himself most are those he faces in his roles as husband and father. Ironically, this nagging doubt will probably be the force that keeps him successful.

" In the most basic sense, I've succeeded. My marriage is intact and my family is provided for. I attend parent-teacher conferences and dance recitals, and my daughters bask in my adoration. And yet, of all the areas of my life, it is in my capacities as a husband and father that I entertain the most doubt. **"**

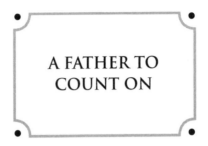

A FATHER TO COUNT ON

IRTHDAY PARTIES ARE a part of life for most little girls. It is such a normal thing that it's funny to think of the leader of the free world putting together goody bags for his daughter's birthday party. Actually, he didn't. Michelle thinks that this is too much responsibility for him and too important to trust to his limited experience. She does trust him to get the balloons, pizza, and ice for the party, though.

Engaging in these ordinary acts of parenting helps Obama close the gap between the idea of parenthood that he holds in his head and what he calls "the compromised reality."

As Malia and Sasha talked with their dad via satellite during the 2008 Democratic National Convention, the world could tell that their father is a real man to them, not a distant, remote global figure. The future world leader is a dad, and a good one at that!

"As I got older I came to recognize how hard it had been for my mother and grandmother to raise us without a strong male presence in the home. I felt as well the mark that a father's absence can leave on a child. I determined that my father's irresponsibility toward his children, my stepfather's remoteness, and my grandfather's failures would all become object lessons for me, and that my own children would have a father they could count on."

A PARENT DEEPLY INVOLVED

WHILE LIVING IN Indonesia, President Obama's mother wanted to ensure that her son grew up knowing the language and culture of his American heritage. When young "Barry," as he was then called, complained to his mother about their 4:30 a.m. homework sessions, Ann Dunham had a firm retort: "This is no picnic for me either, Buster!"

Setting limits with children, invoking discipline, and insisting on structure require true involvement. Kids may think their parents enjoy being "mean." Usually, it is only after children have grown up, made major life accomplishments, or had children of their own that parents are thanked for the structure and discipline they provided. Although, young "Barry" could not appreciate the motive behind those early morning homework sessions, the 44th president of the United States now looks back with admiration and gratitude for a mother determined to position her son to live his best life.

" *There is no policy or program that can substitute for a parent who is deeply involved in their child's education from day one—who is willing to turn off the TV, put away the video games, and read to their child, or help with homework, or attend those parent-teacher conferences.* **"**

OUR JOB AS PARENTS

THE ELECTION OF Barack Obama reflects the aspirations of Americans today, in part, because of the women in his life—wife, Michelle, and daughters, Malia and Sasha. We recognize them as our own—a working woman, wife, and mother like us, and girls like our daughters and granddaughters. They show us ourselves at our best, validate our choices, teach us how to wear the sting of disappointment, and walk in victory with grace.

The Obama women—mother and daughters—reflect a special inner confidence that comes with just being themselves. They send a message that women from every walk of life can accomplish, inspire, and empower by example.

"We want them to grow up with a strong sense of self. We want them to feel that they're being judged on their smarts and their competitiveness and their compassion, and not just, you know, looking cute. So, we talk a lot to them about what values they should be internalizing. Michelle and I agree that our job as parents is really to allow them to make good choices."

THE SUM OF
OUR DREAMS

ONE OF THE few facts that Barack Obama knows about his father is his unwavering belief in the constitutional foundation of America that "all men are created equal." Perhaps this is the source of his belief that as Americans there is no *us and them* in our country, but that we are the *United* States of America.

In his memoir, *Dreams from My Father*, Obama recalls a white single mother of two biracial children living in a mostly black Chicago neighborhood. Her struggles and isolation reminded him of what it was like for his own mother.

Neither the woman nor her children were his responsibility, except he felt a human obligation to help her in any small way that he could. His random acts of kindness to that woman and others led to the trust of many in a community who had grown callous and suspicious of anyone claiming to enter and do good.

"*America is the sum of our dreams. And what binds us together, what makes us one American family, is that we stand up and fight for each other's dreams, that we reaffirm that fundamental belief—I am my brother's keeper, I am my sister's keeper. . . .*"

THE MOST
IMPORTANT JOB

I T'S BEEN A long time since there have been children in
the White House. America's most famous address is a
little more interesting now that Malia envisions doing her
homework at the same desk where Abraham Lincoln signed
what she called "that thing" (a little missive better known as
the Gettysburg Address).

Her parents have affirmed that, yes, there will be sleepovers at
the White House. Surely there will be birthday parties, play-
dates, and visiting friends from Chicago and other places. Who
knows, maybe they'll even pass out Halloween candy from the
White House gates. It's important to Michelle and Barack that
the girls have a real life.

Even though the affairs of the free world pivot around the Oval
Office inside the White House, the Obamas are determined to
give their girls some semblance of normalcy, which is part of
their most important job.

*" Because no matter what you do for a living, we can all
agree that raising our kids and taking care of our
families is the most important job we have. "*

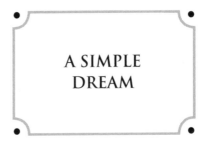

A SIMPLE DREAM

ANN DUNHAM CERTAINLY led an unconventional life, especially for a young white woman in the 1950s and 1960s. She was clearly an amalgam of her adventure-minded father and her quietly determined mother. She was an amazing woman. Her parents surely accomplished what they set out to do—raise a daughter who felt free to live as she chose and to pursue her own dreams. She obviously passed that freedom to pursue one's dreams on to her son.

Obama pursued his dreams indeed. He took a low-paying job as a community organizer on Chicago's South Side that certainly didn't seem to be on a path to fame. His acceptance into Harvard Law School wasn't necessarily a direct path to the White House either. However, Obama's inherited sense of freedom to choose his own fate led him to his destiny. Both his mother, who made what were then radical choices, and his grandparents would be proud to see their simple dreams fulfilled.

" In a time of great uncertainty and anxiety, my grandparents held on to a simple dream—that they could raise
my mother in a land of boundless opportunity; that their
generation's struggle and sacrifice could give her the
freedom to be what she wanted to be; to live how she
wanted to live. "

ANYTHING YOU CAN DREAM

Barack knows the power of dreams. Both his grandfather and father were dreamers. As a biracial boy growing up in Hawaii in the 1960s, it is doubtful anyone told Barack he could be president. However, through the examples of his parents and grandparents, he learned that he could achieve whatever his mind conceived.

Michelle also knows the power of hard work blended with motivation and determination. Her parents modeled the character traits necessary to turn dreams into reality.

Even as our nation places great demands on our first family, this inspirational couple remains focused regarding their most important responsibility. As they draw upon the strengths of their combined experiences, the Obamas will teach their children to dream and to equip themselves with the tools to accomplish those dreams.

" *There's nothing we want more than to nurture that hope; to make all those possibilities and all those opportunities real for our children; to have the ability to answer the question, 'What can I be when I grow up?' with 'Anything you want—anything you can dream of.'* **"**

THE ONE THEY CALL "MOM"

MICHELLE OBAMA IS an accomplished woman in her own right. It's refreshing to know that, with all that she is capable of doing, she chooses to make the Obama girls her number one priority.

Most women in America can relate to putting their children first. Many are working mothers who juggle work and home responsibilities but manage to keep their children a priority.

Malia and Sasha are accustomed to seeing their father on television and in newspapers and magazines, but Michelle is still mainly Mom. Malia got a glimpse of her mother's emerging stature when she saw her photo on the cover of a popular magazine. Malia was impressed because usually they put what she considers "important" people there.

Right now, she's just their mother. However, one day they will know fully the phenomenal nature of the woman they call "Mom."

" When my daughters ask me whether change is possible, I'll tell them that there was a time when a woman who graduated third in her class at one of the most prestigious law schools in the country couldn't find a single firm in America that would hire her. . . . But I'll also mention that years later, the progress made by the women's movement made it possible for Sandra Day O'Connor to leave Arizona and become the first female justice of the United States Supreme Court. . . . And today, if they want to find a female lawyer in a position of prominence, they need look no further than the one they call Mom. "

JOBS THAT HOLD OUR FAMILIES TOGETHER

R AISING A FAMILY IS not easy, even under the best circumstances. Every parent wishes there was someone who could just take the parenting load off for a while. Usually, it is expressed as something like, "I need a break!" When that break comes in the form of grandparents, godparents, family, friends, church folk, neighbors, or others in the community, parents are relieved to have a village to raise their children.

Yet, even without this support system, most parents manage to collect themselves and just do what needs to be done. Even Michelle Obama, "mom-in-chief," has to have steady hands for the many unseen jobs at the family helm as her husband grapples with economic issues and matters of world peace.

❝There are the jobs you do once the workday ends. Jobs like paying the bills, buying the groceries, making the dinner, doing the laundry, enforcing the bedtimes—the jobs you don't get paid for, but that hold our families together.❞

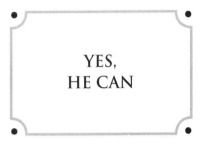

YES,
HE CAN

F OR THOSE WHO know Michelle Obama, they know that her father, Frasier Robinson, had a tremendous impact on her family's story.

On many occasions, Obama has lauded his deceased father-in-law's character and perseverance. Despite a debilitating illness, Frasier Robinson went to work every day for thirty years at Chicago's water filtration plant to support his family. He let nothing daunt his determination to be a good provider for his children. Throughout his life, he provided a modest but comfortable living for his family on the South Side of Chicago.

Because of their hardworking father, both Michelle and her brother, Craig, ventured through doors that had been closed to previous generations.

Men like Frasier Robinson are an inspiration to their children.

"We are the hope of the father who goes to work before dawn and lies awake with doubts that tell him he cannot give his children the same opportunities that someone gave him.

"Yes, he can.**"**

IT MAKES A DIFFERENCE

GOOD PARENTING INCLUDES helping children understand the scope and consequences of their actions and decisions. This takes time, commitment, and consistency. Parenting requires teaching children to make good choices and helping them navigate life's waters—it means not leaving them to sink or swim alone. A family psychologist calls it teaching children to "struggle well." As parents navigate their own journeys, children cannot be left outside the process. Often, kids blame themselves for their family's problems—divorce, loss of job, dwindling income, or the death of a family member. It is so important that they are not left alone to interpret these occurrences.

The Obamas are consistently in touch with what their daughters are thinking and feeling—monitoring their perceptions of the world and the changes going on in their lives.

"It makes a difference when we realize that a child who shoots another child has a hole in his heart no government can fill."

WORTH IT

PRESIDENT OBAMA'S MOTHER and grandparents instilled in him a strong sense of worth. Despite the family's struggles and transitions, he knew that he mattered to his mother, Gramps, and his grandmother Toot.

In *Dreams from My Father*, he recalls the stories his family told him about his father's good qualities. For many years, those stories would give the younger Obama something for which to strive. After one such story, his grandfather leaned over to him, and said, "Now there's something you can learn from your dad. Confidence. The secret to a man's success."

Obama also remembers his grandfather telling him that Americans can do anything once they put their minds to it. He knew his family expected great things from him.

Parents are their children's most powerful motivators to success. They shape their children's sense of themselves in the world and their sense of worth.

"In the end, children succeed because somewhere along the way, a parent or teacher instills in them the belief that they can. That they're able to. That they're worth it."

OUR RESPONSIBILITY AS AMERICANS

SHORTLY BEFORE MICHELLE and Barack married, she traveled with him to Kenya. As he recalls in *The Audacity of Hope*, well into the trip Michelle began to miss the United States. "I never realized how American I was," she said.

"Only in America" is a common phrase. Rags to riches stories abound. People are able to spend their life doing what they choose—whether performing admirable deeds of kindness or vying for fame and fortune.

It is hard to appreciate these things unless you've visited other countries or had conversations with persons who have immigrated here. Unstable governments, dictatorships, military coups, and entrenched poverty are a way of life in many countries.

The realization that, as Obama states, "In no other country on earth is my story even possible," is a truth worth fighting for and passing on to our children.

"As we begin our fourth century as a nation, it is easy to take the extraordinary nature of America for granted. But it is our responsibility as Americans and as parents to instill that history in our children, both at home and at school."

MY FATHER'S IMAGE

MANY KIDS TODAY grow up without a father. However, in the early 1960s and 1970s, not having a father in your life carried an even greater stigma. Young Barack had to contend with an absent father in addition to living in a household where no one looked like him. Plus, he had a funny name. Such challenges undoubtedly leave a child wondering about where he or she belongs.

For a long time, Barack did wonder, though he often kept these thoughts private. Barack was blessed with the mentorship of men of diverse backgrounds who served as role models throughout his childhood and adulthood. He knew these men cared for him and he respected them. Yet as influential as these other men were in his life, they could not placate the longing for his father. Despite their positive and supporting presence in his life, he yearned for his own father. He felt his absence deeply and in ways that still impact him today. In his father's image he saw a reflection of himself, he saw the man that, for a time, he wanted to become.

"*These men had become object lessons for me, men I might love but never emulate, white men and brown men whose fates didn't speak my own. It was into my father's image, the black man, son of Africa, that I'd packed all the attributes I sought in myself, the attributes of Martin and Malcolm, Dubois and Mandela.*"

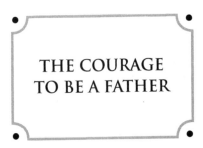

THE COURAGE
TO BE A FATHER

IRST-TIME PARENTS often have a gleam in their eyes. The twinkle in a father's eyes after he looks at his firstborn child is especially endearing. It may come from the pride of having a son to carry on the family name. Or, it may be sparked by the birth of a beautiful baby girl, the epitome of sweetness and innocence, to raise as his own little princess.

Even if the words are never spoken, the adoring look of a father says, "You're loved. You're wanted. You're special. You matter."

We can see it in Barack Obama's eyes when he looks at Malia and Sasha and when he talks about them. The Obama girls know they are special, not because their father is the president of the United States of America, but because he has made them the center of his world, his hopes, and his dreams.

It would be wonderful if all children saw that glow in their father's eyes.

❝There are a lot of men out there who need to stop acting like boys; who need to realize that responsibility does not end at conception; who need to know that what makes you a man is not the ability to have a child but the courage to raise one.**❞**

A CLEANER AND
SAFER PLANET

E VERY GENERATION HAS different kinds of parental concerns, but the dilemmas faced are the same. Parents worry about what the world will be like when their children grow up. They want their children to enjoy the same joys of life they had growing up—eating ice cream in the summer, playing in the neighborhood park, joining Little League or Scouts, attending music lessons, going on first dates, graduating high school, and moving into college dormitories.

Today's parental concerns are similar yet different from just a couple of generations ago—perhaps even compounded. Now, parents wonder whether there will be clean air, pure water, and secure neighborhoods for their children's children. They worry about the damage to the ozone layer and whether crime will wipe out a child's freedom to play in the front yard.

Barack Obama's role as a major world leader, in addition to being a father, only heightens these concerns. In fact, because he is privy to information that the average American does not know, he is motivated even more to build a better world.

" When our children—when Malia and Sasha and your children—inherit a planet that's a little cleaner and safer; when the world sees America differently, and America sees itself as a nation less divided and more united; you'll be able to look back with pride and say that this was the moment when it all began."

A MOTHER'S VOICE, TOUCH

A S A YOUNG child, Barack Obama spent some years living in Indonesia with his mother, his stepfather, and his younger sister, Maya. He embraced this new land and culture with a boyish spirit of adventure and discovery. But he also saw firsthand the hardships and the entrenched poverty endured by men, women, and children living in a developing nation. It was a time of great tumult in Indonesia's history.

It was his mother to whom he turned to make sense of that world. Although she herself was struggling to understand many of the same complexities, her affection and open communication were enough to comfort him. The lessons from these teachable moments with his mother still guide President Obama today.

Obama developed a trusted relationship with his mother that has positively impacted his relationship with his own daughters. His value for the times he spent with his mother is visible in his interactions with his own children.

"Sometimes, when my mother came home from work, I would tell her things I had seen or heard, and she would stroke my forehead, listening intently, trying her best to explain what she could. I always appreciated the attention—her voice, the touch of her hand, defined all that was secure."

LITERACY UNLOCKS GATES OF OPPORTUNITY

ONE OF THE things Malia looked forward to during her father's campaign was the fulfillment of his promise to finish reading one of the latest books in the *Harry Potter* series to her over a single weekend.

It's wonderful that the Obama children appreciate the gift of reading and the entertainment that comes through words. Their interest in reading is probably enhanced by the fact their parents are an active part of their literary endeavors.

A good book can transform a child's imagination. Reading is a gateway to adventure—whether the source is a timeless literary work like Louisa May Alcott's *Little Women* or the latest Spiderman comic book.

Children who grow up in a household where reading is encouraged are more likely to acquire a passion for reading. Trips to the library and local bookstores can also generate a child's interest.

" *In a world where knowledge truly is power and literacy is the skill that unlocks the gates of opportunity and success, we all have a responsibility as parents and librarians, educators and citizens, to instill in our children a love of reading so that we can give them the chance to fulfill their dreams.* "

AMERICA RENEWED ITS PURPOSE

I T IS TRADITION that parents share the joys and trials of an earlier time with their children. Whether recounting stories of the Depression, World War II, an Elvis Presley concert, the Civil Rights Movement, or Woodstock, parents recall events that impress upon their children a generation's place in history.

The milestones of history can serve as landmarks to help future generations determine from where and what their parents and grandparents have brought them. Obama's presidency serves as affirmation—for generations past, present, and future—that change is still possible in America and that it is worth holding on to hope.

Future generations can look back on their parents' and grandparents' actions on Election Day of November 4, 2008, and take pride in how they charted our nation's course in a new direction.

" Someday, someday, if our kids get the chance to stand where we are and look back at the beginning of the 21st century, they can say that this was the time when America renewed its purpose.

" They can say that this was the time when America found its way.

" They can say that this was the time when America learned to dream again. **"**

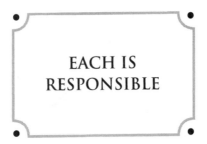

EACH IS RESPONSIBLE

I n *The Audacity of Hope*, Obama recalls a conversation with a successful black entrepreneur whose businesses were mainly on Chicago's West Side. The man lost a leg in the Vietnam War, but didn't use it as an excuse for low ambitions. The two men commented on the changing work ethic of the young people in the area. The businessman noted that they could hardly be expected to stand tall on a foundation that was never built for them.

In this country, no one is excluded from the call to take personal responsibility and to help others along. Whether from a background of privilege or adverse conditions, Americans from coast to coast accept responsibility and use their resources to make better communities and better cities.

Like the Chicago businessman, the beauty of America is that despite obstacles and disabilities, every person has an opportunity to achieve and the responsibility to pass on the benefits of that achievement to their children and their community.

"Each of us, in our own lives, will have to accept responsibility—for instilling an ethic of achievement in our children, for adapting to a more competitive economy, for strengthening our communities, and sharing some measure of sacrifice."

SACRIFICIAL LOVE

WHENEVER MALIA HAS an asthma attack and can't catch her breath, her parents must feel terribly helpless, so they do everything possible to prevent those attacks from happening. And because of their precautions and good medical care, she manages to live a fairly normal life. She plays soccer and enjoys other vigorous activities as well.

Dealing with childhood illnesses is part of parenting—a sometimes terrifying part. First-time parents usually struggle the most. Simple medical issues can render them panic-stricken. As their child grows older, they generally relax and learn to gauge minor ailments from serious conditions.

Feelings of fear over a child's illness are normal and are usually rooted in the parents' sense of powerlessness to help the child they love so much. The gift of these times, however, is the realization of just how sacrificial parental love is.

"I know what it's like to be a parent. And as a father with a little girl who suffers from asthma, I can understand the terror you feel when your child wakes you in the middle of the night gasping for air. When you would rather stop breathing yourself if it meant that she could start breathing just a little easier."

TIME TO READ AND LOVE

R EADING TO HIS girls at night is a treasured occurrence in the Obama household, especially since the opportunities to do so were less frequent during the campaign. No doubt, Malia and Sasha will grow up believing that reading is precious and time well spent. They will always have fond memories of those special moments with their father.

Educators and librarians constantly seek ways to motivate children to read—book clubs, reading contests, and storytelling hours at the local library. Nevertheless, a beloved bedtime story is one of the best ways to nourish the minds of young readers and build solid parent-child relationships. Parents who consistently read to their children a few minutes before bed each night—even those who can't read well or don't have much time to read after working two or three jobs—know the benefit of this quality time. Reading together is making the most of the precious moments parents and children have together.

"And so as parents, we need to find the time and the energy to step in and find ways to help our kids love reading. We can read to them, talk to them about what they're reading, and make time for this by turning off the TV ourselves."

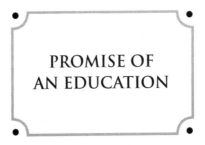

PROMISE OF
AN EDUCATION

I T IS WISELY SAID, "An education is something no one can ever take from you." In America, an education has the power to change one's destiny. The power of education motivated Barack Obama Sr. to leave his homeland to pursue the American Dream and to change his life for the better.

Education gives children high hopes for the future. A child can dream of acquiring an education that will move him or her from poverty to affluence, from powerlessness to influence. Education turns children of sharecroppers into physicians and attorneys. It escalates single mothers from welfare to the ranks of middle-class America. It transforms gang members and drug dealers into legitimate entrepreneurs.

Both Michelle and Barack came from working-class families who encouraged and helped them attain the best education from America's finest institutions of higher learning. They both prove that education yields success.

"In America, it's the promise of a good education for all that makes it possible for any child to transcend the barriers of race or class or background and achieve their God-given potential."

TWO LITTLE GIRLS

BARACK OBAMA'S FAMILY is a central component of many of his speeches. During the campaign, though, he had few opportunities to tuck his little girls into bed at night. Most of their "I love you's" were heard over the telephone or through the television airwaves.

It's tough being a parent with a demanding job. Every parent who has a job that pulls him or her away from family understands the struggle—you want to be with your children, but in order to provide for them you have to be away from them.

Though Malia and Sasha share their father with the entire world, they still realize that he loves them in a special way. Someday, they will reflect on his words spoken at his historic presidential victory speech in Chicago's Grant Park, "I love you both more than you can imagine," and realize the magnitude of his love for them and for the rest of the world.

"*There are two little girls I tuck in at night who deserve a world in which they can dream those same big dreams; in which they can have the same chances as any other child living any other place. It is a dream I share for your children and all of our children, and that is why it's America—always hoping, always reaching, always striving for that better day ahead.*"

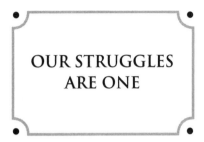

OUR STRUGGLES
ARE ONE

I N HIS RECOUNT of his family gatherings, Obama explains
with amusement that his family reunions look like some
sort of international event. According to him, family members run the gamut in terms of appearance—from Margaret
Thatcher to comedian Bernie Mac. Certainly, his diverse background has taught him that family cannot be defined by race,
color, or culture.

Obama's nontraditional family bloodlines have enabled him to
understand what it means to be part of the human race. He is
strongly connected to his relatives in the rural areas of Kansas,
in the islands of Hawaii, in the remote villages of Indonesia,
and in Kenya where he visited his father's ancestral home and
saw the challenges of his grandmother Sarah Hussein Obama
and other African family members.

If we allow it, our family struggles and experiences can yield a
compassion that helps us understand that we're all intercon-
nected and that we're all part of the human family.

“*Our separate struggles are really one. A struggle for freedom, for dignity, and for humanity. . . . [I]t doesn't matter if [a] child is a Latino from Miami or an African American from Chicago or a white girl from rural Kentucky—she is our child, and her struggle is our struggle.*”

MAYBE I CAN'T, BUT
MY CHILDREN CAN

PARENTS AND GRANDPARENTS invest their hope in future generations. Many lamented Barack's grandmother Madelyn's death just the day before the historic 2008 election. Although she was not able to witness his victory, she was already very proud of her grandson. All that she, her husband, Stanley, and her daughter, Ann, had worked to achieve had come to fulfillment in far greater ways than they could have imagined.

The greatest progress for future generations—regardless of gender, race, or any other limitations—comes when parents and grandparents experience the hopes and dreams of their children.

"Some of us had grandparents or parents that said maybe I can't go to college but my child can; maybe I can't have my own business but my child can. I may have to rent, but maybe my children will have a home they can call their own. I may not have a lot of money but maybe my child will run for Senate. I might live in a small village but maybe someday my son can be president of the United States of America."

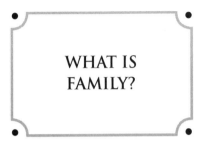

WHAT IS FAMILY?

THE MOSAIC QUALITY of President Obama's family has always been central to his identity—he is in every sense of the word a family man. On the very first trip to visit his relatives in Kenya, and years before he would have a family of his own with Michelle, Barack was crafting a unique definition of family for himself. He yearned to understand its meaning beyond just the biological ties that bond kin to kin.

Perhaps it is because his family was so complex and nuanced—flawed yet lovable, and spread across oceans and continents—that he arrived at a deeper appreciation for his place in their world and their place in his.

Lacking the firm parameters of a traditional nuclear family, Barack broadened his understanding of family to be defined by a less tangible barometer—love, support, nurture, and acceptance.

"What is a family? Is it just a generic chain, parents and offspring, people like me? Or is it a social construct, an economic unit, optimal for child rearing and divisions of labor? Or is it something else entirely: a store of shared memories, say? An ambit of love? A reach across the void?"

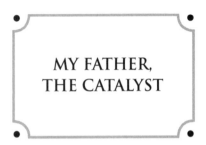

MY FATHER, THE CATALYST

THERE COMES A point in our lives when we wonder if we truly know our parents beyond their roles of mother and father. Most of us are adults by the time we realize that our parents actually had hopes and dreams of their own. What were their ambitions when they were younger? Their triumphs and losses? Their joys and pains?

People who have grown up without a father or mother usually harbor unanswered questions. They tend to create an image of the absent parent, pieced together through memories, stories, and photographs. No matter how elaborate the conjured image, that unfilled place resides in their heart and soul. They try to fill those empty spaces as best they can.

Barack Obama's only real memory of his father's physical presence in his life was a brief encounter that had a profound impact on his psyche—one that left him with more questions than answers. Words left unsaid would continue to haunt him. But it was that interlude that served as a catalyst to finding himself.

"The pain I felt was my father's pain. My questions were my brothers' questions. Their struggle, my birthright."

GRANDPARENT GUARANTEES

G RANDPARENTS TEND TO be less strict and more indulgent with their grandchildren than they were with their own kids. They spoil them while the parents do all the hard work. As they interact with grandchildren, grandparents hardly seem to resemble the same people who insisted on discipline and structure from their own children.

Barack's grandparents, Stanley and Madelyn Dunham, were a major part of his mother's support system and had a considerable influence on his life.

Stanley Dunham had his fair share of life's difficulties. Still, he must have been a phenomenal man. It was at his initiative that his grandson applied for and gained entrance into a prestigious private academy. He wanted to give the boy more than a fighting chance for success. Although they both knew the challenges their grandson would face as a biracial child growing up in the 1960s, Stanley and Madelyn wanted the best for the child they so dearly loved.

"Our parents and grandparents were given no guarantees, and they certainly had their share of failings and hardship, but theirs was a country where if you wanted it badly enough, and were willing to work for it, and take responsibility, you could provide for your family and give your children the same chance. . . . Providing these families with the same chances that previous generations have had is a daunting challenge, but it is certainly one we can meet."

NOW IT'S OUR TURN

M OST AMERICANS HAVE fond remembrances of relatives—the odd uncle with a get-rich-quick scheme, the cousin who is forever trying to land a husband, Grandma's special recipe, and the six-year-old nephew who recites the Gettysburg Address verbatim. Sometimes their memories do not become endearing until these quirky but beloved family members are long gone.

Every generation gains this appreciation once they become senior members of the family and are expected to be the wisest and most giving. They realize that the young people in the family are counting on them to lead the way.

One day Malia and Sasha will grow to appreciate their parents. They will recognize the lengths to which their parents have gone to give them every opportunity for success and happiness and they themselves will take on the responsibility of passing on those values.

"Now it's our turn. It's our turn to make those sacrifices so the next generation doesn't have to. Our turn to open the doors of opportunity that our daughters and grand-daughters will one day walk through."

GRANDMOTHERS' COMMON HOPES

B ARACK'S TWO GRANDMOTHERS grew up worlds apart—
Sarah Obama scarcely left the confines of her village in
Kenya, and Madelyn Dunham lived in various parts of
the United States as her husband chased his fortune.

Both women have something in common—as grandmothers,
they clearly wanted the best for their brilliant grandson. Only
one grandmother, Madelyn, understood the force of the American Dream and could impart it in both word and deed.

Sarah Obama has made her peace with the confines of her
culture. Her grandson quotes her in his memoir *Dreams from
My Father*: "One only knows what one knows. Perhaps if I was
young today, I would not have accepted these things." Unlike
the Dunhams, she had no way of knowing or experiencing the
American Dream. The gift we have in this country to work hard
for our families and ourselves and to go as far as our dreams will
take us cannot be fully appreciated until we encounter those
who have never known the privilege of pursuing dreams.

"*Americans share a faith in simple dreams. A job with wages that can support a family. Health care that we can count on and afford. A retirement that is dignified and secure. Education and opportunity for our kids. Common hopes. American Dreams.*

"*These are dreams that drove my grandparents.*"

THE AMERICAN DREAM IS THE AMERICAN FAMILY

I T IS DEEPLY woven in the American ethos that the next generation is expected to achieve more than their forebears. Therefore, parents work hard to give their children more. But what is *more*, really? It is normal for parents to give their children the things they did not have. But giving more can have a much broader definition.

The Robinsons made a hard choice to live in a small apartment so that Marian could be a full-time homemaker. Without the pressure of an outside job, she was able to instill in Craig and Michelle disciplines and values that are still with them today and impact how they raise their own children.

The two Robinson children have come a long way from their humble beginnings—Craig is head coach at Oregon State University, and Michelle is a respected attorney and First Lady of the United States of America.

The Robinsons' pursuit of the American Dream was to give priority to their American family.

66 *The cost of the American Dream must never come at the expense of the American family.* 99

JUGGLING WORK AND FAMILY

MICHELLE HAS BEEN described by her husband as the "rock" of the Obama family. If she is the rock, then her mother Marian Robinson is the foundation. She's doesn't spend much time in front of the cameras, but America may owe Barack Obama's historic victory to his mother-in-law.

Barack wouldn't run unless Michelle approved. Michelle wouldn't approve unless she knew that she had a firm support system to care for their girls and help keep their lives as normal as possible under the circumstances. At the core of that support system is Marian—the future direction of the free world lay in the hands of a 70-year-old grandmother.

As two-parent incomes become a necessity for most families today, many grandmothers and grandfathers are relieving some of the worry of finding safe and affordable childcare. They are creating lifetime bonds with their grandchildren and allowing working parents to reach higher career goals with peace of mind.

"A child born in this new century is likely to start his life with both parents—or a single parent—working full-time jobs. They'll try their hardest to juggle work and family."

TEACH OUR
DAUGHTERS
THEIR WORTH

B ROUGHT UP IN a disciplined household with very little television viewing, Michelle raises her daughters the same way. As young girls, they have already formed opinions about womanhood based on their own mother. They learn how a woman should be treated by examining their parents' relationship: their father's love for their mother, his generosity and romantic gestures toward her, his respect for her opinions and decisions, and his value of her individuality.

Where did Michelle learn her worth? She examines herself to insure that Frasier Robinson would be pleased with his daughter's behavior and her accomplishments. "I am constantly trying to make sure that I am making him proud—what would my father think of the choices that I've made, how I've lived my life, what careers I chose, what man I married."

" It starts with teaching our daughters to never allow images on television to tell them what they are worth; and teaching our sons to treat women with respect. **"**

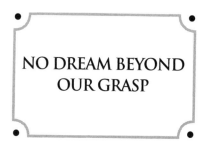

NO DREAM BEYOND
OUR GRASP

MONEY AND STATUS can never buy courage, fortitude, or strength of character. Obama's difficult upbringing cultivated important survival tools that money cannot buy—something important for parents to remember in their quest to fulfill the American Dream.

Instead of dwelling on the absence of a father or isolating himself from a culture struggling to understand what being biracial means, Obama somehow locked into what was most important—love, hope, and the ability to dream.

When his mother divorced his stepfather, Lolo, his half sister, Maya, was only nine. Barack stepped in to offer his little sister what paternal guidance and nurturing he could.

Part of what makes Barack Obama such an intriguing personality is what he has accomplished despite many obstacles. His successes prove that it's the fight in us that determines what we're made of in life.

"I was not born into money or status. I was born to a teenage mom in Hawaii, and my dad left us when I was two. But my family gave me love, they gave me education, and most of all they gave me hope—hope that in America, no dream is beyond our grasp if we reach for it, and fight for it, and work for it."

FAITH AND GUIDANCE

IT HAPPENS WITH every new generation. Parents and grandparents wonder whether the younger generation has gone astray beyond reclamation. For a time, Obama's mother and grandparents worried about him. They did not know the extent of his private struggles, but they recognized and respected the signs of adolescent distance. They needn't have worried, for as he grew older, the seeds sown by his mother and grandparents took root.

More than once he recalled his mother's lessons in empathy: "How would you feel if someone did that to you?" Over the years, her question would replay many times in his head, guiding him to do the right thing. The Dunhams' midwestern pragmatism took hold when he realized he needed to take his education more seriously.

Eventually, we return to the truth that we were taught as children, which is why Obama can smile knowing his parents and grandparents are extremely proud that he is now the nation's 44th president.

"My Bible tells me that if we train a child in the way he should go, when he is old he will not turn from it. So I think faith and guidance can help fortify a young woman's sense of self, a young man's sense of responsibility, and a sense of reverence that all young people should have for the act of sexual intimacy."

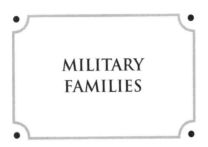

MILITARY FAMILIES

EVERY DAY WE hear news reports about the growing number of American troops deployed to Iraq, Afghanistan, and other parts of the world.

Behind every person deployed is a father, mother, son, daughter, husband, wife, grandmother, or grandfather. Somehow, those left behind find the strength to endure the separation and remain hopeful.

Those who are deployed leave loved ones who must keep their families strong and encouraged. Family responsibilities must be carried out despite a loved one's absence.

Our nation's support for military families is critical because of the toll that deployment takes on the entire family—physically, economically, and psychologically. Even after families rejoice over their loved one's return, they still need support.

Our servicemen and women are serving us, and in the process, their entire families do, too.

"My wife, Michelle, met with Army spouses . . . [a]nd they told her something we all need to remember: 'We don't just deploy our troops overseas, we deploy families.'"

A HOPEFUL WORLD

L ONG BEFORE HE became a husband and father, some South Side Chicago residents who knew Obama wondered why such an educated young black man was working in their community for low pay and no glory.

To those in the academic and corporate worlds who knew him, it was obvious that he had a sharp intellect and bright future. Why then, they must have questioned, was he spending all that potential in a rundown neighborhood?

Obama was raised to believe he had a responsibility to make the world a better place. He wanted to make a difference. This would prove to be more important to him than money or recognition. He had learned from his family that service is the only thing in life that lasts.

Fatherhood seems to have heightened his desire to make a difference in the world. Perhaps it's because if he fails to seize every opportunity to do so, he will one day have to look directly into his girls' eyes and explain to them why he didn't.

"I have two daughters . . . and I can't help but think that they are the reason I wanted to make a difference in this country in the first place—to give them a better, more hopeful world to raise their children."

SPEECHES, WRITINGS, AND SAYINGS BY BARACK OBAMA

Barack. *Dreams from My Father* (New York: Crown, 2004) pg. 220

PAGE 61—THE COURAGE TO BE A FATHER: "Strengthening Families in a New Economy" (Spartanburg, South Carolina, June 15, 2007)

PAGE 63—A CLEANER AND SAFER PLANET: Iowa Caucus Victory Speech (Des Moines, Iowa, January 3, 2008)

PAGE 65—A MOTHER'S VOICE, TOUCH: Obama, Barack. *Dreams from My Father,* pg. 38

PAGE 67—LITERACY UNLOCKS GATES OF OPPORTUNITY: "Literacy and Education in a 21st-Century Economy" (American Library Association, Chicago, Illinois, June 27, 2005)

PAGE 69—AMERICA RENEWED ITS PURPOSE: Emily's List Annual Luncheon (Washington, DC, May 11, 2006)

PAGE 71—EACH IS RESPONSIBLE: Announcement for Presidency (Springfield, Illinois, February 10, 2007)

PAGE 73—SACRIFICIAL LOVE: CURE Keynote Address (Chicago, Illinois, March 11, 2005)

PAGE 75—TIME TO READ AND LOVE: "Literacy and Education in a 21st-Century Economy" (American Library Association, Chicago, Illinois, June 27, 2005)

PAGE 77—PROMISE OF AN EDUCATION: "Teaching Our Kids in a 21st-Century Economy" (Center for American Progress, Washington, DC, October 25, 2005)

PAGE 79—TWO LITTLE GIRLS: "Reclaiming the American Dream" (Campaign Rally, El Dorado, Kansas, January 29, 2008)

PAGE 81—OUR STRUGGLES ARE ONE: National Council of La Raza (Miami, Florida, July 22, 2007)

PAGE 83— MAYBE I CAN'T, BUT MY CHILDREN CAN: Remarks at Campaign Rally (La Crosse, Wisconsin, October 1, 2008)

PAGE 85—WHAT IS FAMILY?: Obama, Barack. *Dreams from My Father,* pg. 327

PAGE 87—MY FATHER, THE CATALYST: Obama, Barack. *Dreams from My Father,* pg. 430

PAGE 89— GRANDPARENT GUARANTEES: "Strengthening Families in a New Economy" (Spartanburg, South Carolina, June 15, 2007)

PAGE 91—NOW IT'S OUR TURN: Remarks at Campaign Rally (Dayton, Florida, September 20, 2008)

PAGE 93—GRANDMOTHERS' COMMON HOPE: "Reclaiming the American Dream" (Campaign Rally, Bettendorf, Iowa, November 07, 2007)

PAGE 95—THE AMERICAN DREAM IS THE AMERICAN FAMILY: "Reclaiming the American Dream" (Campaign Rally, Bettendorf, Iowa, November 07, 2007)

PAGE 97— JUGGLING WORK AND FAMILY: "A Hope to Fulfill" (National Press Club, Washington, DC, April 26, 2005)

PAGE 99—TEACH OUR DAUGHTERS THEIR WORTH: 99th Annual Convention of the NAACP (Cincinnati, Ohio, July 14, 2008)

PAGE 101—NO DREAM BEYOND OUR GRASP: Potomac Primary Victory Speech (Madison, Wisconsin, February 12, 2008)

PAGE 103—FAITH AND GUIDANCE: Call to Renewal Keynote Address (Call to Renewal's Building a Covenant for a New America Conference, Washington, DC, June 28, 2006)

PAGE 105— MILITARY FAMILIES: Campaign Remarks on Veterans (Charleston, West Virginia, May 12, 2008)

PAGE 109—A HOPEFUL WORLD: "Energy Independence and the Safety of Our Planet" (The Associated Press's Annual Luncheon, Chicago, Illinois, April 3, 2006)

PHOTO CAPTIONS AND CREDITS

Atsede Elegba, Photo Editor

PAGE 11—INTRODUCTION: Senator Barack Obama with author following the second presidential debate in Nashville, Tennessee. (October 7, 2008/Photo courtesy Olivia M. Cloud)

PAGE 13—TO HOLD THINGS TOGETHER: President-elect Obama kisses Michelle after addressing supporters at the election night rally in Chicago, Illinois. (November 4, 2008/AP Photo/Jae C. Hong)

PAGE 15— 21ST-CENTURY STANDARDS: Senator Obama, embraces family as they are greeted by supporters in Portland, Oregon. (May 18, 2008/AP Photo/Greg Wahl-Stephens)

PAGE 17—ROCK OF THE OBAMA FAMILY: Obama shares a moment with Michelle during a Hamilton County family picnic. (May 3, 2008/Noblesville, Indiana/© Jason Reed/Reuters/Corbis)

PAGE 19—INSPIRING OUR CHILDREN: Senator Obama blows out candles on his birthday cake at his 43rd birthday celebration with his family during a fundraiser in Matteson, Illinois. (August 4, 2004/Photo by Tim Boyle/Getty Images)

PAGE 21—DIFFERENT STRANDS OF FAMILY LIFE: President-elect Obama hugs Michelle during his election night rally in Chicago. (November 4, 2008/Chicago, Illinois/© Brooks Kraft/Corbis)

PAGE 23—THE SAME OPPORTUNITIES: President-elect Obama and Malia take a break from passing out food at St. Columbanus Parrish and School in Chicago, Illinois. (November 26, 2008/Frank Polich/Getty Images)

PAGE 25—IF KIDS KNOW THEY'RE LOVED: Senator Barack Obama, sits with Sasha during an Independence Day picnic in Des Moines, Iowa. (July 4, 2007/AP Photo/Charlie Neibergall)

PAGE 27—AN IDEAL HUSBAND AND FATHER: Senator Barack Obama, acknowledges the cheers of supporters and receives a hug from Michelle upon arrival at his election night New Hampshire presidential primary rally in Nashua, New Hampshire. (January 8, 2008/AP Photo/Stephan Savoia)

PAGE 29—DREAM WITHOUT LIMIT: Senator Obama and Michelle with Malia, 8, and Sasha, 5, on the front porch of their Hyde Park, Illinois, home before the girls leave for school. (October 2, 2006/Callie Shell/Aurora Photos)

PAGE 31—THE DOUBT THAT BREEDS SUCCESS: Senator Obama attends the Fourth of July parade with his family in Butte, Montana. (July 4, 2008/Credit Callie Shell/Aurora Photos)

PAGE 33—A FATHER TO COUNT ON: Senator Obama and his family enjoy the midway at the Iowa State Fair in Des Moines, Iowa. (August 16, 2007/AP Photo/M. Spencer Green)

PAGE 35—A PARENT DEEPLY INVOLVED: Ann Dunham with her two-year-old son, Barack Obama, Honolulu, Hawaii. (1963/Polaris Images)

PAGE 37—OUR JOB AS PARENTS: Michelle sits with Sasha as they listen to Barack speak to local residents in Oskaloosa, Iowa. (July 4, 2007/AP Photo/Charlie Neibergall)

PAGE 39—THE SUM OF OUR DREAMS: Presidential candidate Senator Obama walks down steps with his children and friends at the National Memorial Cemetery of the Pacific in Honolulu, Hawaii. (August 13, 2008/AP Photo/Alex Brandon)

PAGE 41—THE MOST IMPORTANT JOB: Senator Barack Obama eats shaved ice with his daughters Sasha, 7, and Malia,10, along with unidentified friends in Kailua, Hawaii, for a vacation. (August 13, 2008/AP Photo/Alex Brandon)

PAGE 43—A SIMPLE DREAM: Presidential candidate Obama and his family visit the Iowa State Fair in Des Moines, Iowa. (August 16, 2007/

tor Obama fist-bumps with young Ethan Gibbs at Dulles International Airport in Chantilly, Virginia. (October 22, 2008/Joe Raedle/Getty Images)

PAGE 79—TWO LITTLE GIRLS: Senator Obama stands with Sasha and Malia before speaking to potential supporters in Cedar Falls, Iowa. (August 15, 2007/AP Photo/Charlie Neibergall)

PAGE 81—OUR STRUGGLES ARE ONE: Senator Barack Obama holds his grandmother Sarah Hussein Obama, as they walk alongside family members on during the Senator's visit to his ancestral home in Nyangoma village, Siaya District in Kenya. (August 26, 2006/Nyangoma , Kenya/© JACOB WIRE/epa/Corbis)

PAGE 83—MAYBE I CAN'T, BUT MY CHILDREN CAN: Barack, after his graduation from Honolulu's Punahou School in 1979, with his grandparents Stanley and Madelyn Dunham. (Polaris Images)

PAGE 85—WHAT IS FAMILY?: Maya Soetoro-Ng of Honolulu, half sister of Obama, poses with her husband, Konrad Ng, and their daughter, Suhaila, 2, after meeting with Obama supporters in Honolulu. (May 12, 2007/AP Photo/Lucy Pemoni)

PAGE 87—MY FATHER, THE CATALYST: Malik Obama, older half brother of the president, holds an undated picture of Barack (left), himself (middle), and an unidentified friend in his shop in Siaya in eastern Kenya. (September 14, 2004/AP Photo/Karel Prinsloo)

PAGE 89—GRANDPARENT GUARANTEES: Barack with his visiting grandparents Stanley and Madelyn Dunham, sitting on a bench near Central Park during the time he attended Columbia University in New York, New York. (1983/Polaris Images)

PAGE 91—NOW IT'S OUR TURN: The Obamas, along with Barack's sister, Maya, and her family watch an Independence Day parade in Butte, Montana. (July 4, 2008/AP Photo/Jae C. Hong)

PAGE 93—GRANDMOTHERS' COMMON HOPE: Senator Obama meets his grandmother Sarah Hussein Obama at his father's house in Nyongoma Kogelo village, western Kenya. (August 26, 2006/AP Photo/Sayyid Azim)

PAGE 95—THE AMERICAN DREAM IS THE AMERICAN FAMILY: Craig Robinson sits with his sister, Michelle Obama, at the Democratic National Convention in Denver. (August 26, 2008/AP Photo/Ted S. Warren)

PAGE 97— JUGGLING WORK AND FAMILY: President Obama kisses his mother-in-law, Marian Robinson, during his inauguration as the 44th president of the United States. (January 20, 2009/Chip Somodevilla/Getty Images)

PAGE 99—TEACH OUR DAUGHTERS THEIR WORTH: Michelle stands beside her mother, Marian Robinson, at the Democratic National Convention in Denver. (August 26, 2008/AP Photo/Ted S. Warren)

PAGE 101—NO DREAM BEYOND OUR GRASP: Vacationing Senator Barack Obama talks with his half sister, Maya, as they leave a restaurant in Honolulu, Hawaii. (August 11, 2008/AP Photo/Alex Brandon)

PAGE 103—FAITH AND GUIDANCE: An affectionate moment between Barack's grandfather, Stanley Dunham, and grandmother, Madelyn Payne Dunham, during World War II. (1941/Polaris Images)

PAGE 105—MILITARY FAMILIES: Senator Obama speaks to airmen in Camp Arifjan, Iraq. Senator Chuck Hagel of Nebraska and Senator Jack Reed of Rhode Island joined Obama on his tour of the Middle East and Europe. (July 18, 2008/Photo by Sgt. Brooks Fletcher/U.S. Army via Getty Images)

PAGE 107—A HOPEFUL WORLD: Senator Obama walks down Kailua Beach in Kailua, Hawaii, with Malia, 10, and Sasha, 7, during their vacation in Hawaii. (August 12, 2008/AP Photo/Marco Garcia)